LIFE AT SCHOOL AND IN THE COMMUNITY

Richard Worth

ROSEN
PUBLISHING®
New York

Published in 2010 by The Rosen Publishing Group, Inc.
29 East 21st Street, New York, NY 10010

Copyright © 2010 by The Rosen Publishing Group, Inc.

First Edition

Library of Congress Cataloging-in-Publication Data

Worth, Richard.
Life at school and in the community / Richard Worth.—1st ed.
     p. cm.—(Teens: being gay, lesbian, bisexual, or transgender)
Includes bibliographical references and index.
ISBN 978-1-4358-3580-1 (library binding)
1. Sexual minorities—United States. 2. Teenagers—United States.
3. Coming out (Sexual orientation)—United States. 4. Sexual harassment—
United States. I. Title.
HQ73.3.U6W67 2010
306.760973—dc22

                                                                        2009016588

Manufactured in Malaysia.

CPSIA Compliance information: Batch #TW10YA: For Further Information contact Rosen Publishing, New York, New York
at 1-800-237-9932

CONTENTS

INTRODUCTION

Gay, lesbian, bisexual, and transgender (GLBT) teens deal with important issues in their schools and communities every day. They decide whether or not they want to come out to their peers and family members. They deal with challenges such as harassment and bullying.

Unfortunately, some schools do not have effective programs in place to prevent harassment, or they are not prepared to deal with bullying when it does take place. A negative school environment can impact GLBT students' academic performance. A number of GLBT students even drop out of school in order to avoid being victimized by their peers. For some GLBT teens, finding information and support is a major challenge. Surveys of school libraries indicate that many do not have adequate resources for GLBT teens.

However, things are changing. Today's GLBT teens feel more comfortable coming out and openly expressing pride in who they are. Many schools and communities are more accepting of GLBT teens because of the work that organizations and individuals have done to promote respect, tolerance, and understanding. More and more schools and communities are enacting strict guidelines prohibiting discrimination against any minority group, including GLBT students. Students who participate in bullying or name-calling are disciplined for their actions. Some states have even passed antidiscrimination laws that specifically protect the rights of GLBT individuals.

Thanks to the efforts of proactive GLBT teens and their allies, more and more resources have become available for GLBT students in their schools and communities. With courage and persistence, GLBT teens will be able to surmount any challenges that come their way.

CHAPTER 1

Coming Out at School

Many young people begin questioning their sexuality by the age of twelve or thirteen. You may be questioning yours, too. Some teens discover that they are gay, lesbian, or bisexual. Others discover that they are transgender, meaning that they identify with a gender different from that of their biological sex. And still others discover that, ultimately, they are heterosexual. Every person is unique, and there is no age by which you need to define who you are.

A person's sexual orientation is defined by who he or she is romantically and sexually attracted to. People who are attracted to members of the opposite sex are said to be heterosexual, or straight. Those who are attracted to members of the same sex, or of both sexes, are said to belong to the GLBT community.

A person's biological sex describes whether he or she is physically male or female. Biological sex, however, is different from gender. A person's gender is ultimately decided by whether that person feels more like a male or female. The gender that a person identifies with is known as his or her gender identity. Transgender people have a gender identity that is different than that of their biological sex.

When GLBT teens or adults make their sexual orientation or gender identity public, it is known as "coming out." Not all GLBT teens choose to come out to their classmates. Some wait until they are out of school before coming out. Others might only come out to their parents, a trusted member of the school staff, or a close friend.

If you are a GLBT teen, it can be difficult to know exactly when and how to come out. While you want to fit in and feel accepted by your classmates, you do not want to be false to your own values and beliefs. It is no good winning acceptance if you have to pretend to be someone that you are not. It is also likely to make you feel uncomfortable and anxious. Even if you decide not to come out right away, the most important thing is to be true to yourself. The struggle to define oneself is among the most difficult tasks that face any teenager, especially a GLBT teenager.

Defining Who You Are

For GLBT teens, the road to identity and self-discovery can be difficult. Even at a very young age, some people know that they

Coming out at school can be difficult because you don't know how your peers might react. However, living openly as a GLBT individual, and not having to pretend to be someone you're not, can be very rewarding.

have a sexual orientation or gender identity that is different from most of their peers. Others might have a very different experience. They may be unsure about their sexual orientation or gender identity at first. There is no single path to learning whether or not you are GLBT. The important thing is to be honest with yourself and to not expect that you will have all of the answers right away.

It can be easy for GLBT teens to feel different in a sea of heterosexual peers. And it is easy to worry about not fitting in, or not being accepted by other students. If you are a GLBT teen, you may wonder what your classmates, teachers, coaches, and counselors might think of your sexual orientation or gender identity. You may worry that other students will harass or bully you. You may wonder if you will find other teens who are questioning their sexual orientation as well. You might also wonder what kinds of programs, groups, and organizations there are in your school and community that are aimed at teens like yourself. Everyone's situation is different, and there is no way to predict how people will react until you actually come out.

Coming Out at School

There is enormous diversity among GLBT teens. The timing of how or when to come out to teachers, classmates, and peers is different for each member of the GLBT community. According to Caitlin Ryan, director of adolescent health at San Francisco State University, the average age range for coming out used to be from nineteen to twenty-three. Today, the average age range for coming out has dropped considerably. Many GLBT teens come out when they're in junior high or high school.

Today's GLBT teens often feel more comfortable telling friends who they are because these days society is more accepting of GLBT people. More heterosexual young people will accept someone of another sexual or gender orientation with little or no hesitation. This does not mean that GLBT teens no longer face discrimination and bullying. However, American culture has changed a lot from a generation ago, and GLBT teens and adults are more likely to be up front about their sexual orientation or gender identity.

If you want to come out to your friends, it is important that you wait until you feel comfortable doing so. The right time to come out varies from person to person, and not everyone is ready to come out right away. However, just as it can be difficult to come out, it can also be difficult to keep your sexual orientation or gender identity a secret. Some GLBT teens may be comfortable coming out to their peers because it allows them to decide when and where to tell others in school who they are.

Examples of Coming Out

There are many ways you can come out to your classmates. A February 2005 article in the *Advocate* profiles students who successfully came out to their peers. One sixteen-year-old girl with a supportive group of friends came out to them as bisexual. The girl explained to them that she was a very independent teenager who had always done what she thought was right. For her, that meant coming out to her friends and telling them that she was a bisexual teen. She felt that it was very important to be honest with them, and she did not want to pretend to be someone she was not. Her friends supported her decision to come out, and they treated her exactly as they did before.

A middle school boy chose a different way of explaining who he was: he put it in writing, and then he read what he had written to the class. His written piece revealed the fact that he was gay. It was his way of telling everyone who he really was. The boy was comfortable with his sexual orientation, and he felt it was important that his friends understood that he was not heterosexual.

These two young people made an important decision to come out to their peers. Much like the teenagers in these examples, many GLBT teens have supportive friends, families, and peers. Others are not so lucky. Some teens feel confident about coming out to their peers at school, while others might wait until they move away from home, or until they graduate from high school and find a GLBT community at college. Only you can decide when and how to come out to your peers.

If you decide to come out at school, it is natural to feel some anxiety as you approach the moment of truth. As you prepare to tell others about yourself, rehearse what you might want to say. Try it out with a friend or sibling who may already know that you are a GLBT teen. Then select a small group of people with whom you feel especially close. Pick a good time to come out, when they will not be distracted by something else.

Do not be surprised if everyone does not respond to your announcement with a positive reaction. Remember that any negative reactions you receive have nothing to do with you. Some people are uncomfortable with anyone whose sexual orientation or gender orientation is not the same as theirs. Their discomfort may come from the fact that they are afraid of people who are

This couple met at a support group for GLBT teens. GLBT organizations can assist GLBT teens who want to come out to their peers.

different from them or because they are uncertain about their own sexual orientation or gender identity. Others may not immediately accept your sexuality, but they may eventually understand and value you as a person. Although their reaction may be disappointing, it is important to be patient and give them time. Remember that you cannot change your sexual orientation or gender identity to fit someone else's expectations.

In his book *Sexual Politics*, Shannon Gilreath recalls an incident when he was in graduate school. Gilreath, who was openly gay, said he was "received well" by his classmates. "I became the unique person everyone wanted to know ... I was welcomed by everyone." Everyone, that is, except for a student who tried to avoid him. This student rebuffed all of Gilreath's efforts to be friendly. At the end of the year, a few days before graduation, Gilreath was playing pool with some of his friends. Suddenly, he saw this student approaching him.

This Wisconsin GLBT student group holds a meeting during lunchtime at their school. Even in an accepting school environment, it's normal to worry about your peers' reaction when you come out.

At first, he expected to be insulted, but he was surprised at what his classmate had to say. "I just wanted you to know," the young man confessed, "that before I met you, I couldn't conceive of having a gay friend. But having known you, I see what I've been missing by automatically dismissing everyone who is different from me." By simply being himself, Gilreath had an impact on other students. As his fellow student told him, "The school needs more people like you."

No matter how accepting a group of friends might be, it is normal to worry about their reaction when you come out. This emotional conflict is experienced by many GLBT teens. In *Sexual Politics*, Gilreath talks about this conflict and the risks of not coming out. While it might seem safer to keep one's sexual orientation or gender identity a secret, Gilreath points out that doing so robs people of their dignity. "Ultimately, we make the choice to be other than we are, to remain less than whole," he says. He explains that people who do not come out may be concerned with "self-maintenance, preserving both private and public life with as few scrapes and bruises as possible. But truly living," he adds, "is about more than mere self-preservation; it is about cultivating the best within us."

Some students have an especially supportive school environment and are lucky enough to have the support of most of their teachers and peers when they come out.

Unfortunately, this is not the case for all GLBT teens, and it might not be the case for you. However, you may also discover that you have many friends in school who accept you as a person and as a GLBT teen. To them, you are just their good friend, no different than you ever were, and they are there to support you. These are the people with whom you want to spend your time. They are the ones who recognize that it took courage for you to take a risk and tell others about yourself. And they will form a community of people with whom you can really be yourself.

CHAPTER 2

Life at School

It is not always easy being different from most of your peers. GLBT teens live in a society that is predominantly heterosexual. Social events at your school are primarily designed for heterosexual teens. Films and television programs largely feature representations of heterosexual couples dating and falling in love. To date, most states ban gay marriage, and the federal government does not recognize same-sex marriages. If you are a GLBT teen, you may feel that no one else understands what you are going through, or that no one really knows who you are. You may feel cut off from your peers and even your family.

You need support, understanding, and acceptance to feel comfortable among the majority of your peers. Social support networks of like-minded people are crucial for teens, both straight and GLBT. That is why school organizations like Gay-

Straight Alliance (GSA) chapters are so important. Not only do they give gay and transgender teens a chance to be themselves, they also allow them to be among people who know what they are going through, who understand their feelings, and who empathize with them.

Gay-Straight Alliances

The idea for GSAs originated in the late 1980s with a gay man named Kevin Jennings. At the time, Jennings was a high school teacher in Boston. He found himself counseling a gay student who was very depressed. The student felt that no one seemed to understand him. In 1988, Jennings spoke at a school assembly about being gay, which generated interest among some of the students. One of them was a straight girl with a lesbian mother. She told Jennings that it was time to start a club for gay students. Her family was regularly being ridiculed in school. According to the Web site of the Gay, Lesbian and Straight Education Network (GLSEN), the student told Jennings, "I'm straight and you're gay, so let's call it a gay-straight alliance." Jennings would go on to found GLSEN shortly afterward, in 1990.

In the two decades since the first Gay-Straight Alliance was established in Boston, GSAs have flourished in schools across the country. As of April 2009, there were more than 4,400

Many GLBT teens find support from a chapter of the Gay-Straight Alliance (GSA) in their school. Seen here are members of a GSA based in a Florida high school.

registered GSAs in the United States, according to GLSEN. While GSA chapters can't be found at every school, new GSAs are being formed each year. Sympathetic peers, as well as understanding teachers, can be great allies in school. If your school does not have a Gay-Straight Alliance chapter, you and your friends may want to consider starting one.

Establishing a GSA chapter is one way that GLBT students can organize to prevent bullying. It allows them to take control of the situation, instead of letting the situation control them. However, GLBT students can meet with resistance from school adminis-trators when trying to set up a GSA. Some administrators may not be familiar with GSAs. Others may not support the efforts of GSAs to create a safer, more welcoming atmosphere for GLBT students in school. If

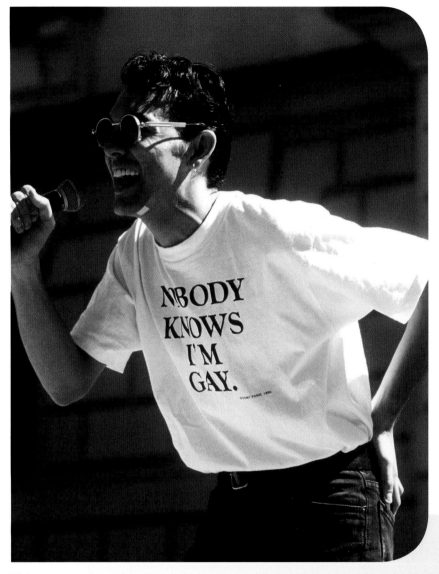

This young man addresses a crowd at a National Coming Out Day rally in Texas. It takes courage to let others in your school know that you are gay or lesbian.

the school will not give you any assistance in setting up a GSA, you can often receive help from organizations like GLSEN or a local chapter of Parents, Families and Friends of Lesbians and Gays (PFLAG). You can also contact GLSEN to schedule a program at your school about bullying and how it can be prevented. In addition, GLSEN runs seminars and workshops about GLBT teens, breaking down stereotypes, and promoting understanding among straight students.

It takes courage for students to step up, let others know who they are, and take the lead in establishing an organization for others like them. Doing so, however, can be very rewarding. Many students have found a strong community in their school's GSA. They report feeling safer after joining because they no longer feel alone. Some teens feel more empowered to stand up to bullies, and to report threatening or harassing behavior. GLBT students who are members of GSAs say they feel more connected to other students at their school. If you join a GSA, you may find that you can feel a greater connection to school staff. You may even take a leading role in your school's GSA, becoming president of a local chapter and participating in GSA and GLSEN awareness events. You can even help establish GSA chapters in other schools and even speak at school assemblies about your group's goals and activities.

A GSA chapter at your school can lead a celebration of GLBT History Month. This occurs each October, with a

GLBT Teens in the Media

For many years, people were afraid to let others know that they were GLBT. This was especially true in the media. During this time, many GLBT actors, actresses, and other public figures were afraid to come out for fear of how it might affect their careers.

In recent years, this has changed. For example, in 1994, a gay character named Ricky began appearing on the television program *My So-Called Life*. The actor who played Ricky, Wilson Cruz, was openly gay himself. In 1997, *Ellen*, the first show to feature a gay central character, appeared on TV. Today, GLBT teens can be seen on many network and cable television programs, including MTV's *Real World* and *Degrassi: The Next Generation*. Books dealing with GLBT topics can be found in libraries across the country, including many public school libraries. Young people routinely reveal their sexual orientation or gender identity on online social networking sites like Facebook. Online GLBT media has flourished, and virtually every GLBT organization has an online presence. Today more than ever, GLBT teens and adults have a voice in media.

National Coming Out Day on October 11. GLSEN sponsors No Name-Calling Week to help eliminate the taunting of GLBT students, as well as an annual Day of Silence. The Day of Silence initiative began at the University of Virginia in 1996. Since that time, an estimated five hundred thousand students

Many people believe that same-sex marriage should be legal. Thanks to popular support, many states are legalizing same-sex marriage, as well as passing other legislation that will benefit GLBT individuals.

at approximately four thousand public schools and colleges annually participate in the event, according to GLSEN. Students enlist the support of teachers and school administrators for the Day of Silence. As part of the event, students may remain silent for the entire day or just selected parts of it, such as lunch. They do so to highlight how GLBT students are silenced in schools by harassment and bullying. They may also participate in Breaking the Silence activities, like student rallies.

Ten Great Questions to Ask a School Guidance Counselor

1. **What kind of resources do you have for GLBT students?**

2. **How can I establish a GSA in my school?**

3. **Are there any teachers that would be interested in serving as advisers?**

4. **Are there any teachers interested in setting up a safe zone in their classrooms?**

5. **What kind of scholarships am I eligible for as a GLBT teen?**

6. **How can I tell if a college I am interested in has GLBT groups and organizations on campus?**

7. **Is there a way for me to anonymously report bullying?**

8. **Is there anything I can do to prevent cyberbullying?**

9. **Who should I talk to if I'm experiencing depression?**

10. **Are there any resources in the community for GLBT teens?**

Beyond High School

In his book *The New Gay Teenager*, Ritch Savin-Williams wrote that the best colleges are looking for bright, talented, GLBT students "because of these young people's assumed moxie, toughness and resolve." These students have taken the risk to come out among their peers, join support groups, and let others know who they are. According to Savin-Williams, colleges believe this reflects the students' "self-confidence, leadership abilities, and cultural awareness." Currently, there are numerous GLBT organizations and support groups at colleges across the country.

If you are a GLBT student, there are scholarships available for you. For instance, the Point Foundation identifies successful GLBT scholars and awards them scholarships of up to $30,000 per year. Founded in the late 1990s, it is dedicated to providing financial support to exceptional GLBT students. By doing so, it hopes to promote tolerance. The Point Foundation also offers community support to GLBT students. Each year, it holds a retreat for its scholars. The retreat includes boat rides on the Great Lakes and discussion groups. In addition, scholars are given adult mentors to help them chart a path for themselves in college and a career after graduation.

The message is clear: if you are a GLBT teen, you are not alone. There are support groups for you to join, colleges

Colleges are eager to accept students who have taken the risk and come out. These students gather at a GLBT booth at Columbia University in New York City.

that want to accept you, and scholarships for you and teens like you. The GLBT community has entered the mainstream, where it is finding greater acceptance. GLBT teens and young adults are forming groups in high schools and colleges in order to achieve common goals. Now more than ever, it is possible for GLBT teens to come out and feel comfortable being themselves.

CHAPTER 3

ENCOUNTERING PROBLEMS AT SCHOOL

While the environment at many schools has become more welcoming for GLBT teens, serious problems still exist. According to GLSEN's 2007 National School Climate Survey, approximately 86 percent of GLBT students reported being the object of name-calling because of their sexual orientation. Nearly 45 percent of GLBT students experienced harassment that crossed the line and became physical, and 22 percent experienced outright physical assault. Even if it is not directed at a particular student, abuse can still be quite hurtful. Among students, 90 percent heard someone use the word "gay" to describe things that are considered to be bad or negative. Harassment can create such a negative or harmful environment for GLBT students that it can actually affect their grades. According to the National

Part of the Hetrick-Martin Institute in New York City, Harvey Milk High School provides a safe and supportive environment for both straight and GLBT students.

Mental Health Association, gay, lesbian, and bisexual teens may be as much as four times more likely to drop out of school than their heterosexual peers.

Harassment and Bullying

Even GLBT teens with supportive school environments are unlikely to find that all of their classmates accept their sexual orientation or gender identity. According to GLSEN, 83 percent of GLBT students reported being called names or threatened because of who they are. GLSEN also revealed that some GLBT students got nasty comments from school administrators or teachers. GLBT students are more than four times as likely to skip school because they want to avoid threats or taunts from their peers.

Transgender students can be particularly singled out for bullying and harassment. According to GLSEN, nearly every transgender student—approximately 90 percent of those surveyed—had negative language directed at them from other students. Much like gay and bisexual teens, transgender students were more likely to avoid school or skip classes to avoid abuse.

Many people—both teachers and students—may not be well informed about issues relating to gender identity and expression. Transgender students may also have difficulty finding books and other resources in their school or local library that cover issues related to gender identity. Ignorance

Freedom of Expression

The First Amendment to the U.S. Constitution protects your right to free speech and free expression. The government is not allowed to violate this right. These rights extend to you in your school and your community.

In a public school, you cannot be prevented from coming out to your classmates. If you attend a public school without a dress code, you should not be prevented from wearing a shirt that expresses your sexual orientation or gender identity. Your First Amendment rights ensure that you should be permitted to hold hands with a same-sex friend or bring a same-sex friend to a school event, such as a dance. However, these rights generally do not cover harassment. That is to say, other students should not be allowed to express themselves by verbally or physically harassing GLBT students.

about GLBT issues can make it harder for school staff to identify and stop abuse, and it can make it easier for bullies to act the way that they do.

Dealing with Bullies

While some schools may be more supportive than others, and some geographical areas more accepting than others,

Many GLBT students suffer in silence at school. This mother looks at pictures of her child, who took his own life at the age of fourteen after struggling with his sexual orientation. It's important to talk with someone, such as a school counselor, if you are feeling seriously depressed.

harassment can rear its ugly head in the most unlikely places. In an interview with *Boston Globe* reporter David Abel about establishing a GSA chapter, Kevin Jennings said, "It is the best of times and the worst of times. The level of support is higher than ever before. But at the same time, these students are disproportionately at risk for violence and harassment. Now they're increasingly visible and a bigger target."

So what can a GLBT teen do about bullying and abuse in school? One approach that will not work is to do nothing when you are the target of harassment. Harassment is a form of bullying, and it is important to speak up and identify the bully. Bullying will not stop as long as the bullies think they can get away with it. Bullies like the power they feel from picking on anyone who seems weaker than they are. They also crave the attention they receive from others who agree with them and join in the bullying tactics.

When confronted by a bully, it is best to ignore him or her and simply walk away if you can. Some people stand firm and face down the bully. They tell that person to stop. If this does not work, they quietly confront the bully without getting into an argument. If the bully still doesn't stop, it is best to walk away from the person and his or her friends, especially if you are fearful of physical abuse. Make sure you report the bullying incident to someone in the school administration or to a teacher. It can be a good idea to report

This Texas high school student won a battle to establish a GSA in her school. She is seen here with her parents.

abuse to a teacher or another staff member who seems to be sympathetic to GLBT teens.

You may be able to determine which teachers will be sympathetic by simply listening to their comments in class or outside the classroom. Your school may have safe zone stickers on several classrooms. These rooms are identified with a pink triangle or a rainbow, indicating that the teacher is sympathetic to anyone who is having issues because of his or her differences, especially GLBT teens.

Unfortunately, not all students feel comfortable reporting abuse or intimidation to school staff. According to GLSEN's 2007 National School Climate Survey, only about 60 percent of students reported abuse to a school staff member. Transgender students were slightly less likely to report physical and verbal abuse. The survey also stated that school staff responded to only about 70 percent of reported abuse. If an unsympathetic teacher is indifferent to you when you report abuse, do not give up. There is no reason why you should have to tolerate bullying.

Policies Against Bullying

Different schools take different approaches in their policies on GLBT teens and bullying. Most have policies on harassment and bullying that include GLBT students. In Boulder, Colorado,

Many colleges and universities have established GLBT student services. These students gather in the GLBT student services office at the University of Vermont.

Casey Middle School presents a program at the beginning of each year that explains that the harassment of any student is strictly prohibited. Anyone caught violating this rule is immediately disciplined by school administrators.

"I still don't believe it's safe for eleven- to fourteen-year-olds to come out without support," explained Alison Boggs, principal of Casey Middle School, in a 2008 interview with ABC News. The school makes a special effort to ensure that GLBT students have a safe environment. It also has counselors to help those who decide to come out.

Some schools have set up bully boxes in an attempt to stop this form of harassment. These boxes enable students to anonymously report a bullying incident or a situation in which

Equal Access

Generally, there are two types of school clubs: curricular and non-curricular. Curricular clubs relate to a subject that is taught in the classroom; a history club, for example. Noncurricular clubs relate to subjects that are not taught in the classroom; for instance, there can be a bird-watching club. Gay-Straight Alliances are non-curricular clubs.

The Federal Equal Access Act, passed in 1984, states that all noncurricular clubs must have the same rights. This means that if noncurricular clubs are permitted to exist in your school, the school cannot refuse your request to start a GSA chapter. In addition, the Equal Access Act says that if a school allows one club to be featured in the school yearbook, put up posters, hold meetings, recruit members, make announcements, or otherwise promote its activities, all other clubs must be given the same rights. This includes GLBT clubs like GSAs. The American Civil Liberties Union (ACLU) points out that if your school tries to prevent you from starting a GSA chapter, you can appeal to the law.

one teen helped another deal with bullying. Students fill out a form describing the nature of the bullying, and they place it in the box. Generally, students are more likely to report bullying or intimidation if they can do so privately.

Stopping Bullying

The American Civil Liberties Union (ACLU), an organization that defends individual civil rights, recommends that GLBT students go to the principal or school guidance counselor to report bullying and abuse. In addition, it recommends that GLBT students keep a written record of what happened when they were bullied, including the date, time, students involved, and description of the incident. According to the ACLU, federal courts require schools to respond to incidents in which GLBT students are harassed or bullied.

If the school does not deal with the problem, the ACLU recommends that GLBT teens get in touch with one of their local offices. Founded in 1920, the American Civil Liberties Union has more than five hundred thousand members and supporters, and it has offices in all fifty U.S. states. The organization has been a powerful force in getting academic institutions to stop harassment, often without taking them to court. Some students find support from the news media. Local news outlets are sometimes willing to publicize the efforts of GLBT teens who are trying to form organizations or otherwise stand up for their rights. This type of coverage can draw attention to GLBT students' activities, increase support for their cause, and put pressure on schools to recognize the needs of all GLBT teens.

These California high school students are represented by the ACLU after filing a lawsuit against their school. They claim that articles on GLBT issues were censored in their school newspaper.

Teens who go to an outside organization for help might find themselves the center of attention in a struggle for GLBT rights. Sometimes, this publicity and attention is unwanted. Students who go to organizations like the American Civil Liberties Union may find that their peers, as well as members of their school's faculty and administration, may not like what they are doing. However, they may also find that many other people in their school—both students and teachers—support them.

Books and School Libraries

School libraries provide an important link between students, their community, and the world. Libraries bring in a vast amount of information that enables all students—not just

Schools and libraries need resources that accurately portray GLBT teens. These resources provide important support and a link to the community of GLBT young people.

GLBT students—to understand different viewpoints and broaden their own horizons. Unfortunately, some school libraries do not have many GLBT resources.

Books and trusted online resources are extremely important when you are trying to understand who you are and learn from the experiences of people who have confronted the same issues you are facing. Reading helps you realize there are other people out there who are just like you. They have confronted the same problems and, in many cases, learned how to successfully deal with them. Reading can also be an effective way to lessen your feelings of loneliness.

The proper resources can work to bridge the gap between GLBT teens and their straight peers. Most stereotypes are rooted in ignorance. The more that students are educated in GLBT teen issues, the less likely they may be to engage in bullying. Without access to these resources, students, schools, and communities suffer.

Some individuals and organizations do their best to prevent school libraries from carrying books on GLBT topics. However, they are seldom successful. It can take courage to defend your rights, but you will find that it is often the best solution. This can mean working with other GLBT students, as well as with supportive teachers, librarians, and administrators to create an academic environment that is free from discrimination and allows you to blossom to your fullest potential.

CHAPTER 4

GLBT RESOURCES IN THE COMMUNITY

Fifteen years ago, Dan Kelly cofounded Outspoken, a community youth group in Norwalk, Connecticut. Kelly works with a number of GLBT students, some of who have been victims of harassment. His youth group provides a place where teenagers can learn how to deal with harassment when it occurs. "If [GLBT teens] are targeted before they come out," Kelly says, "then it can really be difficult for them. My experience has been that gay boys are more likely to get targeted than lesbian girls."

In Connecticut, there is a law that guarantees everyone the right to a safe school, and this includes GLBT teens. A second law instructs teachers to show respect and compassion for all of their students. "Laws," Kelly points out, "really change attitudes." At schools, he adds, safe zones and GSAs help GLBT kids know that support is there for them if they need it. Even if GLBT teens don't regularly attend their school's GSA or take

This Nevada high school student *(left)* was harassed at school after coming out. He sued his school district and won a large settlement. His school district agreed to implement policies to protect GLBT students.

advantage of safe zones, it can still be helpful for the teen to know that these resources are there.

The same applies to community GLBT organizations. Kelly's group meets from 4 to 6 PM each Sunday at a gay and lesbian community center. The group discusses a variety of topics, including coming out, dating, and part-time jobs. Some members' parents have had a difficult time dealing with their child's sexual orientation. So the group discusses this problem. "Coming out is a process," Kelly says. Many of the kids are out to a few friends, and then the word spreads and more people hear about them. By contrast, Kelly adds, "other kids take on a very activist role in school and try to make changes."

GLBT community organizations have been established in towns and cities across the United States. If you are interested in finding an organization in your area, you should probably talk to friends and teachers. Some GLBT teens may feel shy about attending a program at a GLBT community center. This shyness is quite natural. Many of those who attend may also be shy. Perhaps some of them have not come out yet, or they have come out and encountered hostility. Still, GLBT community programs provide a safe environment in which to discuss common issues and solve problems that arise in school or at home.

Problems Outside of School

No one can deny that GLBT teens face challenges in their communities as well as their schools. A 2007 study by the National Gay and Lesbian Task Force Foundation states that about 20 to 40 percent of all homeless youth in America—an estimated 1.6 million of them—are GLBT teens. Some of

GLBT students often find that the support of groups like GSAs help them get through difficult times. These students are gearing up for the Gay/Straight Youth Pride march in Boston, Massachusetts.

them—an estimated 26 percent—were ordered to leave home by their parents when they came out. Others became homeless as a result of escaping conflict or abuse in their household or to escape harassment in youth shelters and foster homes. GLBT teens who have been forced to live on the

Many GLBT students find support from their peers. Strong friendships can help teens avoid depression.

streets are more likely to engage in risky sexual behavior, such as unprotected sex. Being homeless puts GLBT teens in a vulnerable position, and they may be taken advantage of or abused. Some homeless GLBT teens turn to drugs or alcohol.

Just as a disproportionate number of GLBT teens are homeless compared to their straight peers, GLBT teens can be more likely to suffer from depression and other mental health issues. It is important for GLBT teens to remember that even if they don't have a support network at the moment, there are people out there who are willing to help them.

GLBT teens who feel alone, misunderstood, or victimized for being GLBT often look for ways to escape from their situation. Some turn to drugs or alcohol, which can lead to dependence. GLBT teens are almost 200 percent more likely to use drugs and alcohol than their straight peers, reveals a study by Dr. Michael P. Marshal of the University of Pittsburgh Medical Center, which was published in 2008 in the journal *Addiction.* "Homophobia, discrimination, and victimization are largely what are responsible for these substance use disparities in young gay people," Marshal says. "It is important to remember that the vast majority of [these] youth are happy and healthy . . . More than anything, [they] need love, support, and acceptance from their family members and friends."

Substance abuse can have serious consequences. Not all the effects of substance abuse may be visible at first, but the

Meeting Supportive Peers

It is extremely important for teens to connect with like-minded friends and peers. GLBT organizations and groups can help GLBT teens meet others like them. For instance, GLSEN holds a conference called PrideWorks every year in Hudson Valley, New York. When the conference began, no GLBT teens attended—only adults who counseled these students in school. According to a December 16, 2007, article in the *New York Times*, an estimated three hundred teens from the area attended by 2007. Many went with their parents. Students who attended had the opportunity to participate in a variety of seminars, such as "Coming Out—How, When, Where?," "Gay-Straight Alliance in Middle School," and "What Is Transgender?" The event gave them an opportunity to meet other people and deal with the loneliness that they might have felt in their schools.

truth is that abusing drugs and alcohol is detrimental to your physical and psychological well-being. Substance abuse can also impact your performance in school and thereby jeopardize your chances of getting into a good college or university. Substance abuse can also make it likelier for all teens to engage in unprotected sex, placing them at a higher risk for contracting sexually transmitted diseases (STDs). It can lead to depression, physical harm, and, if untreated, addiction. There are many resources for teens struggling with substance abuse, such as support groups and treatment programs. And there is evidence that teens who have supportive social groups may be less likely to engage in substance abuse at all.

Finding Resources

In most schools and communities, there are many resources that exist to help GLBT teens. These may include a sympathetic teacher with a safe zone in his or her classroom, a school guidance counselor, a pediatrician, a GSA chapter in your school, or community organizations in your town or city. Most GLBT organizations offer resources and contact information online.

Teens living in urban and suburban areas are more likely to locate GLBT resources than those in rural areas. Some GLBT teens living in rural areas may not have access to the Internet in their homes. And public and school libraries might have software that filters out GLBT content. There may not be any other GLBT students who have come out in school, and it is possible that no straight students would be interested in joining them in a GSA.

A teacher who is willing to establish a safe zone in a classroom can make a big difference for rural GLBT youth. A GLBT student interested in forming a GSA but who is unable find peers interested in joining can look into joining a GSA at a neighboring school district. If this is not possible, community colleges may provide a solution. Many GSAs at community colleges will allow high school students to attend meetings. Finding a social network is very important for GLBT

In Fort Lauderdale, Florida, both teachers and students gather at a GLBT community center. They are organizing a GLBT-sensitivity training program for school staff.

teens, even if it involves looking outside of one's school.

Organizing Events and Meetings

If GLBT organizations do not already exist in your school or community, you and your friends may want to consider developing them. If you would like to start your own GLBT organization, there are many resources out there that can help you do so. You can also talk with people in GLBT community organizations about their experiences starting and running a GLBT group.

If you decide to form a GLBT organization outside of school, talk to people in the community—such as town administrators, librarians, or community center directors—to find out if they will provide the space and time for you and your friends to hold events or meetings.

If you are interested in starting a GSA or other organization, you should:

- Determine who would be interested in starting a group or organization with you.
- Decide, as a group, what kind of organization you want to form and what your goals are. If you are interested in starting a GSA in your school, contact GLSEN for information.
- If you are starting a school organization like a GSA, you may have to register it with your school. Inform the school administration of your intentions. Your school may require a faculty member to act as a sponsor of each school club. It is a good idea to look for a faculty member who understands the importance of establishing a GSA chapter at your school. If you are starting a community group, you may want to ask an adult to act as an adviser for your group.
- Come up with a name for your group.
- Establish a meeting place for your group. If you are forming a GSA, find a place in the school to hold meetings. If you are forming a different kind of

This Bay Shore, New York, couple is planning to go to the Pride Gala, a prom for GLBT youth. GLBT organizations can be started not only in your school but also in your community.

organization, locate places in the community, such as the public library, which host meetings for other organizations. Be prepared to talk about the group that you want to start, your goals for the group, and when you want to hold meetings.

- Hold regularly scheduled meetings that everyone can participate in.

If you are starting a GLBT group in your school or community, you will want to organize meetings and events that will be successful. Well-organized meetings have a greater chance of attracting a large number of attendees. First, you should discuss an event that fits your organization's goals. Perhaps you might invite a speaker who will talk about some of the key issues that face GLBT teens. Or you might schedule a film screening that relates to the mission of your organization. Make sure the event encourages participation by as many attendees as possible. For example, arrange a discussion after the film or leave time for your audience to ask your speaker questions.

Be sure to promote your event so that others will hear about it. Promotion might include an article in the local newspaper, handing out fliers, and putting posters on bulletin boards at your school and in other locations—such as libraries, churches, and supermarkets—where people are likely to see them. Always ask for permission before putting up posters. The more publicity you can get, the more likely you are to have a successful event.

CHAPTER 5

CREATING

POLITICAL CHANGE

In 2008, young people became involved in unprecedented numbers in the presidential campaign of Democratic senator Barack Obama. They attended rallies, went door-to-door soliciting support, and, if they were old enough, cast a ballot for their candidate. They helped Obama become the first African American to be elected president of the United States. His election showed the effectiveness of grassroots support, especially among young people.

Some students become actively involved with the GSA chapter at their school or participate in a Day of Silence. Others join community centers for GLBT teens, march in parades, and lobby state legislators to support antidiscrimination laws. However, not all of us are political activists. For example, you may quietly support GLBT issues while deciding to come out only to a few close friends.

Political action in the community is one effective way to safeguard your rights as a GLBT teen. This GLBT teen speaks at a news conference about discrimination that he has faced.

rights when it comes to renting an apartment, buying a house, or using public recreational facilities.

Some states have passed antiharassment laws that protect GLBT students. California, for example, passed the Student Safety and Violence Prevention Act of 2000. Before the law was passed, many schools believed that GLBT students were responsible for being harassed by their straight peers, says Carolyn Laub, executive director of the state's Gay-Straight Alliance Network. Under the new law, GLBT teens can require their schools to prohibit harassment and discipline students who engage in it. In Washington State, an antiharassment bill sponsored by Representative Ed Murray was passed by the state legislature in 2002 after a five-year battle.

Being Proactive

There are many ways that you can support legislation protecting GLBT rights. Some GSA chapters try to influence state legislators to pass laws that protect the rights of GLBT students. You can write your state legislators to support antidiscrimination laws if they do not already exist in your state. You can support national organizations, such as the National Gay and Lesbian Task Force, which are working to end discrimination. Or you can just register to vote and support candidates who favor pro-GLBT rights legislation.

Harvey Milk High School

Harvey Milk High School, named after prominent gay politician Harvey Milk, is the United States' first GLBT-oriented high school. First established in New York City in 1985, Harvey Milk High School was envisioned as a place where GLBT students could pursue a high school education free from bullying and harassment from homophobic students and administrators. To date, the school has been a major success. Nearly all students who attend it graduate, and the majority of them go on to pursue a college education. Many of the students attending Harvey Milk High School transferred there after facing abuse at the schools they had previously attended. The school is also open to non-GLBT students. Besides offering a supportive learning environment, Harvey Milk High School also provides a number of programs for students. These range from health and wellness programs to college prep programs.

The progress that GLBT teens and adults have made can be directly traced to their efforts at promoting tolerance in schools and communities. While much still needs to be accomplished in order to eliminate anti-GLBT discrimination, the GLBT community has made significant gains. Many GLBT teens are comfortable coming out because they know they will have support from their peers, GLBT organizations, and

If you checked "no"
complete this form.

VOTER DECLARATION—Read, sign, a
I am a U.S. citizen, will be at le_ _ 18 year
not imprisoned or on parole for a
the laws of the State of California

SIGNATURE—You must s

All U.S. citizens can register to vote when they turn eighteen. Taking an active role in local politics is a great way to get involved in your school and community.

schools. Society has become more accepting, thanks in large part to young people willing to tolerate and respect GLBT individuals. Whether you choose to get involved politically, or just make a statement by quietly being true to yourself, you will help make the world a safe, more welcoming place for GLBT teens, adults, and families.

Myths and Facts

Myth: No one will help me establish a GLBT group at school.

Fact: Talk to sympathetic members of the school staff if you are having a hard time establishing a GSA. Even if you can't find resources in your school library, there are trusted organizations with online presences like GLSEN, PFLAG, the Human Rights Campaign, and the National Gay and Lesbian Task Force that you can get in touch with. Check for groups and organizations in your community. If there are none, you can always get in touch with groups in neighboring communities.

Myth: Colleges are not interested in accepting GLBT students.

Fact: Colleges are absolutely interested in accepting GLBT students. In fact, any experience you might have from getting involved in GLBT issues at your school or in your community will only make you a more attractive candidate to college recruiters.

Myth: You will always feel like an outsider.

Fact: There are almost certainly other GLBT teens in your school and community. There are many resources out there for you. And no matter what your situation is, there are people who are willing to offer you support. You just have to find them.

#

allies People, organizations, or other entities that join forces for a common purpose. The word "ally" is often used to describe a heterosexual individual who supports the GLBT community.

bisexual A term used to describe people who are attracted to members of both sexes.

bullying Intimidating, harassing, or otherwise being cruel to another person.

coming out The act of making one's sexual orientation or gender identity public.

cyberbullying A form of bullying conducted electronically through cell phones or the Internet.

discrimination Treating a person unfairly based on his or her race, nationality, gender, sexual orientation, gender identity, or other characteristic.

gay A term used to describe men who are attracted to other men. It is also used to describe anyone who is attracted to members of the same sex.

gender identity A person's conception of whether he or she is male or female. A person's gender identity can be different from his or her biological sex.

harassment Any kind of behavior that is intended to bother a person. Harassment can include verbal taunts or threats, bullying, and other forms of abuse.

ignorance A state of being uninformed or uneducated about something.

lesbian A term used to describe a woman who is attracted to other women.

peer For teens, a peer is someone who is of the same age or from the same grade level.

recourse The act of turning to an individual or entity for assistance.

rural A term used to describe an area that is not urban or suburban.

safe zone An area in a school, often a teacher's classroom, where GLBT students can feel safe from harm.

sexual orientation A term used to describe who a person is attracted to, be it members of the same sex, opposite sex, or both sexes.

stereotype A generalization about people based on the group or class they belong to. Stereotypes are generally rooted in ignorance.

tolerance The act of respecting people's differences.

transgender A term used to describe individuals whose biological gender does not match their gender identity.

For More
Information

CAEO Quebec

Case postale

55505 Succ Maisonneuve

Montreal, QC H1W 0A1

Canada

(888) 505-1010

Web site: http://www.caeoquebec.org

This organization maintains a Gay Line and Gay Online program to answer questions from GLBT teens.

Gay, Lesbian and Straight Education Network (GLSEN)

90 Broad Street

New York, NY 10004

(212) 727-0135

Web site: http://www.glsen.org

GLSEN is an organization dedicated to ensuring safe schools for all students.

Gay-Straight Alliance Network

1550 Bryant Street

San Francisco, CA 94103

(415) 552-4229

Web site: http://www.gsanetwork.org
This organization provides support for establishing local GSA chapters in schools.

Human Rights Campaign (HRC)

1640 Rhode Island Avenue NW

Washington, DC 20036-3278

(800) 777-4723

Web site: http://www.hrc.org
The HRC is the United States' largest GLBT civil rights organization.

National Gay and Lesbian Task Force

1325 Massachusetts Avenue NW

Washington, DC 20005

(202) 393-5177

Web site: http://www.thetaskforce.org
This organization is dedicated to promoting civil rights for GLBT individuals.

Parents, Families and Friends of Lesbians and Gays (PFLAG)

1726 M Street NW

Washington, DC 20036

(202) 467-8180

Web site: http://www.pflag.org
PFLAG is dedicated to providing information and support for parents and other family members of gay and lesbian individuals.

PFLAG Canada

1633 Mountain Road

Box 29211

Moncton, NB E1G 4R3

Canada

(888) 530-6777

Web site: http://www.pflagcanada.ca

PFLAG Canada provides information and assistance to Canadian GLBT individuals and their families.

The Trevor Project

9056 Santa Monica Boulevard, Suite 208

West Hollywood, CA 90069

(310) 271-8845

Web site: http://www.thetrevorproject.org

The Trevor Project provides a twenty-four-hour crisis hotline for GLBT youth.

Web Sites

Due to the changing nature of Internet links, Rosen Publishing has developed an online list of Web sites related to the subject of this book. This site is updated regularly. Please use this link to access the list:

http://www.rosenlinks.com/glbt/school

For Further READING

Burns, Kate, ed. *Contemporary Issues Companion: Gays and Lesbians*. Farmington Hills, MI: Greenhaven Press, 2005.

Gold, Mitchell, and Mindy Drucker. *Crisis: 40 Stories Revealing the Personal, Social, and Religious Pain and Trauma of Growing Up Gay in America*. New York, NY: Greenleaf Press, 2008.

Howe, James. *Totally Joe*. New York, NY: Atheneum Books, 2005.

Jennings, Kevin. *Always My Child: A Parent's Guide to Understanding Your Gay, Lesbian, Bisexual, Transgendered, or Questioning Son or Daughter*. New York, NY: Simon & Schuster, 2003.

Johnson, Maureen. *The Bermudez Triangle*. New York, NY: Razorbill, 2004.

Keen, Lisa. *Out Law: What LGBT Youth Should Know About Their Legal Rights*. Boston, MA: Beacon Press, 2007.

Leviathan, David. *Boy Meets Boy*. New York, NY: Knopf, 2003.

Marcus, Eric. *What If Someone I Know Is Gay?: Answers to Questions About What It Means to Be Gay and Lesbian*. New York, NY: Simon & Schuster, 2007.

Sanchez, Alex. *So Hard to Say*. New York, NY: Simon & Schuster, 2004.

BIBLIOGRAPHY

Abel, David. "Despite Gains, Gay Teens Still Targets of Violence." *Boston Globe*, April 20, 2003. Retrieved March 2009 (http://www.gaypasg.org/gaypasg/PressClippings/2003/April%20 2003/Despite%20gains,%20gay%20teens%20still% 20targets%20of%20violence.htm).

American Civil Liberties Union. "What's Your Problem?" ACLU. org, March 1, 2007. Retrieved March 2008 (http://www.aclu. org/lgbt/youth/28754res20070301.html).

Arce, Rose. "Classes Open at Gay High School." CNN.com, September 8, 2003. Retrieved March 2009 (http://edition. cnn.com/2003/EDUCATION/09/08/gay.school).

Caldwell, John. "Gay Straight Revolution." *Advocate*, June 21, 2005.

Cloud, John. "The Battle Over Gay Teens." *Time*, October 2, 2005. Retrieved March 2009 (http://www.time.com/time/printout/0,8816,1112856,00.html).

CNN Interactive. "Gay Teens Finding More Support Amid Hostile School Hallways." CNN.com. Retrieved March 2009 (http://www.cnn.com/HEALTH/9901/25/gay.teens).

Edwards, Holly. "Gay Teens Struggle to Find Support at School, Form Alliances with Peers." Tennessean.com, March 8, 2003. Retrieved March 2009 (http://www.one-in-teen.org/documents/article_030803.pdf).

Elias, Marilyn. "Gay Teens Coming Out Earlier to Peers and Family." *USA Today*, February 7, 2007. Retrieved March 2009 (http://www.thetaskforce.org/TF_in_news/07_0222/stories/1_usatoday_gayteenscomingout.pdf).

Gilreath, Shannon. *Sexual Politics*. Akron, OH: University of Akron Press, 2006.

GLSEN. "The GLSEN Jump-Start Guide: Building and Activating Your GSA or Similar Student Club." GLSEN.org. Retrieved March 2009 (http://www.glsen.org/binary-data/GLSEN_ATTACHMENTS/file/000/000/974-1.pdf).

GLSEN. "The 2003 National School Climate Survey." GLSEN.org. Retrieved March 2009 (http://www.glsen.org/binary-data/GLSEN_ATTACHMENTS/file/300-3.PDF).

GLSEN. "The 2007 National School Climate Survey." GLSEN.org. Retrieved March 2009 (http://www.glsen.org/binary-data/GLSEN_ATTACHMENTS/file/000/001/1306-1.pdf).

Holzman, Winnie. "In My So-Called Life." *Advocate*, July 19, 2005.

James, Susan Donaldson. "Young Teens Openly Express Sexuality; LGBT Preteens Proud, Not Safe." ABC News, July 16, 2008. Retrieved March 2009 (http://abcnews.go.com/print?id=5381271).

Johnson, Ramon. "Coming Out Step-by-Step." About.com. Retrieved March 2009 (http://gaylife.about.com/od/comingout/ss/comingout.htm?p=1).

Kelly, Dan (cofounder, Outspoken), in discussion with the author, March 2009.

Lehoczky, Etelka. "Young, Gay, and OK." *Advocate*, February 1, 2005.

Lobron, Alison. "Easy Out." *Boston Globe*, November 11, 2007. Retrieved March 2009 (http://www.boston.com/bostonglobe/magazine/articles/2007/11/11/easy_out?mode=PF).

McBride, Hugh. "Gay Teens Turning to Drugs & Alcohol." TeenDrugAbuse.org. Retrieved March 2009 (http://www.teen-drug-abuse.org/gayteens_alcoholdrugs.php).

Mental Health America. "Factsheet: Bullying and Gay Youth." Retrieved March 2009 (http://www.nmha.org/go/information/get-info/children-s-mental-health/bullying-and-gay-youth).

Randel, Derek. "A Bullying Program for Schools." StoppingSchoolViolence.com. Retrieved March 2009 (http://www.stoppingschoolviolence.com/articles/InSchool/articles_School_bullyPrg.html).

Ray, Nicholas. "Lesbian, Gay, Bisexual, and Transgender Youth: An Epidemic of Homelessness." National Gay and Lesbian Task Force Policy Institute and the National Coalition for the Homeless. Retrieved March 2009 (http://www.thetaskforce.org/downloads/HomelessYouth.pdf).

Savin-Williams, Ritch. *The New Gay Teenager*. Cambridge, MA: Harvard University Press, 2005.

Tussing, Melissa. "Students Take Vow of Silence to Protest LGBT Discrimination." NorthbyNorthwestern.com, April 19, 2007. Retrieved March 2009 (http://www.northbynorthwestern.com/2007/04/2970/silence/?print=true).

University of Pittsburg. "University of Pittsburg Media Release: Gay Youth Report Higher Rates of Drug and Alcohol Use." AddictionJournal.org, March 25, 2008. Retrieved March 2009 (http://www.addictionjournal.org/viewpressrelease.asp?pr=74).

Welter, Kim. "Testimony of Kim Welter Before Ohio Senate Education Committee Regarding H.B. 276." SafeSchoolsToledo.org, December 12, 2006. Retrieved March 2009 (http://www.safeschoolstoledo.org/welteret_sstestimony.htm).

Wessler, Stephen. "Discrimination Against Gay, Lesbian, Bisexual and Transgender Individuals in Maine." Center for the Prevention of Hate Violence, October 2005. Retrieved March 2009 (http://www.preventinghate.org/pdfs/glbt.pdf).

Whelan, Debra Lau. "Out and Ignored: Why Are So Many School Libraries Reluctant to Embrace Gay Teens?" *School Library Journal*, January 1, 2006. Retrieved March 2009 (http://www.schoollibraryjournal.com/article/CA6296527.html).

Winerip, Michael. "For Gay Teenagers, Hope in Numbers." *New York Times*, December 16, 2007. Retrieved March 2009 (http://www.nytimes.com/2007/12/16/nyregion/nyregionspecial2/16Rparenting.html?_r=1&scp=1&sq=prideworks&st=nyt&oref=slogin).

INDEX

About the Author

Richard Worth is an award-winning author who has written more than fifty books for young adults. These include books on family living and self-help. This is his second book for Rosen Publishing.

Photo Credits

Cover Queerstock.com; cover (inset) © www.istockphoto.com/James Pauls; cover (background and border), pp. 1, 4 Shutterstock.com; p. 8 © Steve Skjold/PhotoEdit; pp. 12–13 krtphotoslive/Newscom; pp. 14–15, 20–21 krtkidselements/Newscom; pp. 22, 66 © Bob Daemmrich/PhotoEdit; p. 25 Justin Sullivan/Getty Images; pp. 28–29 © Lee Snider/The Image Works; p. 31 Mario Tama/Getty Images; pp. 34, 54–55 krtphotos/Newscom; pp. 36, 42–43, 47, 57, 62 © AP Images; pp. 38–39 Jordan Silverman/Getty Images; p. 44 Jupiterimages/Workbook Stock/Getty Images; p. 49 © Marilyn Humphries/The Image Works; p. 50 showcasepix/Newscom; pp. 65 © www.istockphoto.com/kledge.

Designer: Les Kanturek; Photo Researcher: Cindy Reiman